Pat Burne

Gallery Books
Editor: Peter Fallon

THE O'NEILL

Thomas Kilroy

THE
O'NEILL

Gallery Books

The O'Neill
is first published
simultaneously in paperback
and in a clothbound edition
on 26 October 1995.

The Gallery Press
Loughcrew
Oldcastle
County Meath
Ireland

© Thomas Kilroy 1995

ISBN 1 85235 163 2 (*paperback*)
 1 85235 164 0 (*clothbound*)

  The Gallery Press receives financial assistance from An Chomhairle Ealaíon/The Arts Council, Ireland.

Characters

The Irish
HUGH O'NEILL, Earl of Tyrone, called The O'Neill
CORMAC, his brother
ART, his illegitimate brother
MABEL BAGENAL, his third wife
ROISIN, his courtesan
POET
CLANSMEN and CLERICS
PATRICK M'ART MOYLE, First Spy
GILLABOY O'FLANNIGAN, Second Spy
THADIE MAHON, Third Spy

The English
SIR ROBERT CECIL, Secretary of State
LORD MOUNTJOY, Lord Deputy of Ireland
MASTER MOUNTFORT, an English preacher on the Irish side
SECRETARY
COUNCIL MEMBERS

Time and place

The play is set in Ireland and London before, during
and after O'Neill's victory at the Yellow Ford, 1598.

Act One
The Battle of the Yellow Ford and the years before.

Act Two
The Battle of the Yellow Ford and the years after.

The O'Neill was first produced at the Peacock Theatre, on Friday, 30 May 1969, with the following cast:

HUGH O'NEILL	Joseph O'Connor
CORMAC	John Kavanagh
ART	Frank Grimes
MABEL BAGENAL	Bernadette McKenna
ROISIN	Joan O'Hara
POET	Alan Devlin
PATRICK M'ART MOYLE	Edward Byrne
THADIE MAHON	Dermot Kelly
GILLABOY O'FLANNIGAN	Tom McGreevy
SIR ROBERT CECIL	Patrick Duggan
LORD MOUNTJOY	Aiden Grennell
SECRETARY	Patrick Dawson
MASTER MOUNTFORT	Joseph Pilkington
HARPIST	Marese Dolan
OTHERS	Seamus Newham
	Desmond Ellis
	Louis McCracken
	Eddie Lynch
	Michele Lohan
	Deirdre Lawless
	Barry O'Kelly
	Seamus Brennan
	Jack Kelly
	Catherine O'Rourke
	Marcella O'Riordan
Director	Vincent Dowling
Design	John Ryan
Music	Gerard Victory

for my son, Hugh Kilroy

ACT ONE

A simple representation of a battle-field. Upstage, on platforms, a tent-like structure. Pikes stand upright beside it. To the side, also upright, is the standard of Fitzmaurice: SPES NOSTRA, JESU ET MARIA. *The Yellow Ford. A great battle has just been fought.* O'NEILL *stands centre, surrounded by* ART, CORMAC *and his clansmen.* MASTER MOUNTFORT *occupies a prominent position. Drum-beat.*

O'NEILL Read out our claims now, Master Mountfort, so that everyone may know what Ireland demands.

MOUNTFORT The claims of O'Neill, Prince of Ulster, given out at the Yellow Ford in the heat of this great victory over the English:

> One: That the Catholic, Apostolic and Roman religion be openly preached and taught throughout Ireland as it was in times past.

> Two: That there be erected a university upon the crown rents of Ireland, wherein all sciences shall be taught according to the manner of the Roman Catholic Church.

> Three: That O'Neill and O'Donnell with all their partakers may peaceably enjoy all lands and privileges that did appertain to their predecessors two hundred years ago.

> *Enter* CECIL *and* MOUNTJOY, *well downstage, on an apron.*

CECIL (*Exictedly*) Stop! Stop! This can't go on. Utopia! Utopia! (*To* MOUNTJOY) This fellow O'Neill means

11

to be king of all Ireland. (*Waves a document*) Listen further to this.

MOUNTJOY (*Reading*) Four: That all statutes made against the preferment of Irish be rescinded.

CECIL Absolute treason, Mountjoy.

MOUNTJOY Oh, it was to be expected, wasn't it? I mean this is war, my lord, not just a minor riot.

CECIL But this fellow would set himself up in place of the Queen. Listen to this —

MOUNTJOY My lord, you will get this at the climax of all rebellions.

CECIL You are cool, for someone who has just been appointed Lord Deputy of Ireland to stamp this out.

MOUNTJOY Quite the contrary. I was never as confused in my life. But at least I can recognise the danger when I meet it. But I am confused. I am still confused by O'Neill and his Irish wars. Do you think we might possibly begin at the beginning again?

CECIL (*Irritably*) I thought we had covered all that.

MOUNTJOY Perhaps just once more. I cannot be content until I have everything clear in my head. I like facts. They are my friends.

CECIL (*Grudgingly*) Very well. (*Aloud to the assembly*) Let us begin at the beginning once more, please. Everybody now. (*There is a disgruntled murmur from all present*)

O'NEILL Must I go back over all that, again?

CECIL I'm afraid so. We must go back once more before we can go on.

> O'NEILL *gestures wearily and his followers disassemble the set and depart, leaving him alone with* MOUNTJOY *and* CECIL.

(*Clearing his throat before recitation*) Now, Hugh O'Neill, Earl of Tyrone, called The O'Neill by the Irish in their ancient fashion. Son of Matthew, Baron of Dungannon. Befriended by Our Majesty and taken at an early age from his savage origins, he was lodged in our country with Leicester for his betterment, education, the surroundings of courtly manners, and a civilized language. I've often wondered about the advisability of educating our future enemies —

O'NEILL Must we go back so far again? I am nearly fifty years of age. I had forgotten so much.

CECIL (*Persistent*) However, however, he returned to Ulster where, against all our expectations, he has become the match to set the country aflame, threatening all progress with this monstrous rebellion of his.

MOUNTJOY My lord, you move too quickly for me. I have some questions —

CECIL Just a moment, Mountjoy. Make a note of this point which I have just now made. This little veneer of civilization makes O'Neill the more formidable an enemy. Watch it. This man has learned our ways. He has brought back with him into the mists and slush of Irish forests a germ of the greatest civilization since the Caesars.

O'NEILL Bull!

CECIL I beg your pardon, sir!

O'NEILL You English insist on taking credit even for the rebellions which succeed against you.

CECIL (*Angrily*) I repeat. This man is dangerous only in so far as he has imposed our ideas on his savage race.

O'NEILL (*With a great roar*) We fight for the cause of unity, unity of all Irishmen under a common Gaelic culture, language and law. Unity of Europe under Rome. The resurrection of Christendom. The healing of the wound made by the wolf Luther.

CECIL (*To* MOUNTJOY) Religion has something to do with it, of course. It always has, with those Irish. But it is essentially a problem of development. The old decayed world of the Irish must be replaced by a new order. It is a rule of nature that the weak must give way to the strong.

O'NEILL (*In wonder*) It is a cause of great holiness, beauty, simplicity.

CECIL Strategy, my dear Mountjoy. You must use the

right tactics on these Irish.

O'NEILL Can we not begin now?

CECIL (*To* MOUNTJOY) Strategy, my lord. Pay particular attention to brothers. They are notoriously ambitious and will slit one another's throats at the mere promise of a title.

MOUNTJOY Brothers?

CECIL Yes, brothers. Cooks and doctors may enjoy greater opportunities for assassination but brothers are the more dedicated to hate. You see an Irishman's blood is not like ours, my lord. It is fat with unnatural substances which break out like boils in fierce passion and temper. Altogether an easy victim for the man of patient mind, don't you think?

O'NEILL Lies! That is no longer true. All Ireland is out. There is a great army on the march, a great brotherhood. Even the centuries of the dead are marching with us.

CECIL My dear O'Neill, you know perfectly well that your people can be split by one hard word in anger, by the jingle of coins.

O'NEILL It is not true. We are a new nation, under our own natural leaders. We will be proud of our freedom.

CECIL Your people are no more fit for self-government than the black savages of hot countries. You will find that they will betray you behind your back.

O'NEILL We will see.

MOUNTJOY Let us begin, please.

CECIL Very well. I call up first the three spies.

O'NEILL No, not that. Not that!

CECIL Thadie Mahon! Patrick M'Art Moyle! Gillaboy O'Flannigan!

Enter the three, silhouetted at the back. They present an ominous tableau.

O'NEILL I will not look at them. Get them out of here. They are the shame of their race. They are the insects that feed on dung. I will not look at them. I will not look.

Exits unsteadily.

I will not look.

MAHON   (*Forward to audience*) Me name is Thadie Mahon. I have a wee business up in Newry. Not much, mind you, but we make ends meet, thanks be to God.

MOYLE   (*With a bow*) Patrick M'Art Moyle appointed by Her Majesty to be Sheriff and Custodian of the Peace in the County of Monaghan, at your service.

O'FLANNIGAN   Hello, hello. The name's Gillaboy O'Flannigan but me friends call me Gill.

CECIL   These are our eyes and ears, Mountjoy. Through them I have watched O'Neill grow until he became the cock of today. I have watched and listened to him even in his Dungannon, plotting with his Jesuits and his Spaniards. Listen.

MAHON   Times is hard. 'Tisn't easy, let me tell you, to make a living nowadays. 'Tis well for them that have money and cattle. They're alright, so they are. It's the poor people like ourselves have to earn it hard. You never know where the money goes but it all adds up, pennies here, pennies there.

MOYLE   Everybody knows the good service which I and my family have done the country. My post is one of importance, if I say so myself. I have been consulted often by the Council in Dublin and have seen the best of society. I have sat in the Commons of Ireland. The wife and I have been introduced to the Lord Deputy himself as he rode by in the Castle Yard. We've worn English clothes all our lives. You might say I'm one of the new ruling class of Ireland.

O'FLANNIGAN   I likes to feel at home with people. Everybody knows me. Skip the introduction I always says. From Carrickfergus to Dundalk, Drogheda to Dublin, they all know me. Everywhere I go I'm treated as one of the lads. I suppose I'm a bit of a boyo in me own way. I like me jar. Never refused a drink from anyone yet, priest or sailor, Christian or blackman. Never refused the offer of a bed either. Especially if the husband's away. Ha! Ha! I have to

15

have it regular, God help me. Still take me or leave me, as they say. I don't ask for favours. Maybe Gillaboy O'Flannigan's no saint but he's no slave neither.

CECIL Speak, spies. This is what you are paid for.

ALL THREE (*In monotone*) What is O'Neill to us? Don't we have to make a living for ourselves like everyone else? What is O'Neill to us?

MAHON Yis. Ye'd like some word of O'Neill, is it? (*Looks around furtively*) They say — they say he's only waiting for a Spanish invasion and he'll drive the English into the say (*sea*) and crown himself a King above in Dublin Castle. God help us but his hand is on the shoulder of every man in the country. He'll be the end of us yet.

O'FLANNIGAN I declare to Christ all this is the gospel truth. You want my advice? Give the buggers enough rope and they'll hang themselves. Who the blazes do they think they are, anyway? The O'Neills! A scatter of English and a cannon would make bits of them all in next to no time.

MOYLE I can speak for the better class of citizen in the country. We are waiting for the arrival of the new Lord Deputy, Lord Mountjoy, to squash this upstart. God save the Queen!

CECIL You have some loyalists among the natives, my lord.

MOUNTJOY I distrust them. Now, where does all this leave us? O'Neill occupies all Ireland: a King, only without a crown. He has just lately destroyed Bagenal at the Yellow Ford. And ten years ago he was a loyalist. The question is why? What devil suddenly possessed him in middle age? (*Muses*) The arch traitor. The Great Running Beast as he is known at court.

CECIL My dear Mountjoy, you exaggerate the fellow's importance. You are fighting a decayed society and not one man. His people, their customs, their ignorance, their pettiness will destroy O'Neill for you. You have only to use them.

MOUNTJOY I must first discover the devil that encountered O'Neill ten years ago.

CECIL   Actually, you know the trouble really started some time before that. Thirteen years ago, to be exact, when we made him an earl. Earl of Tyrone. I always find that the Irish really become troublesome when they gain office and position. What do you think?

MOUNTJOY   My experience of them is limited.

CECIL   Hah! It is! It is! That will soon be rectified. Yes, thirteen years ago. Come, my dear fellow, let us go back. We'll see. We'll see whether it is just one man we have to deal with. Or something less mortal.

> *They leave. As the spies speak a set is lowered. The interior of O'Neill's fort at Dungannon. A low hanging ceiling of rough wood and wattles. Door centre, facing audience. A single, rug-covered seat occupies a central position.*

MOYLE   It is eleven years ago. The place: Dungannon of the O'Neills. O'Neill professes loyalty to the Crown, but judge for yourselves.

MAHON   (*Breathlessly*) They say he's secretly drilling. That he has machines in a cellar for making bullets. That he has all kinds of yokes stored away waiting for the rebellion.

O'FLANNIGAN   Listen here. A pal of mine explained it all to me the other day. It's this way, ya see. O'Neill is happy on his arse above in Dungannon as long as the English don't bother him. But 'tis vice versa with the clansmen who're all for blood and whatever they can lay their hands on.

MOYLE   If I and others on the spot had been listened to then, no one would have been fooled. But the experts in Dublin always know better. Have a look and judge for yourselves.

> *They exit in a line.*
> *Pipe music and drums. Enter an aisle of sullen clansmen carrying torches. The* POET, *who stands aside.* O'NEILL *enters with* CORMAC *and* ART. *He is alert and active at thirty-seven years of age, distin-*

guished from the others by his earl's costume, elabo-
rate doublet and hose, glittering buckled shoes, a hat
with gorgeous feathers. All the others wear rough
Irish mantles and the traditional glib. O'NEILL *seats*
himself.

CLANSMAN 1 O'Hagan, son of Art, son of Con, of the fosterers of the O'Neills, brings to you, Hugh O'Neill, the strength of his right hand, a hundred head of cattle and thirty bowmen, ten of them out of the Western Islands of Scotland.

CLANSMAN 2 O'Quinn, Son of Neel, brings to you —

O'NEILL Alright. That'll be enough now. I have something to say to you and then you may all go off home. Listen carefully and carry back my words to the clansmen beyond sight of Dungannon. (*Loudly*) I am now Earl of Tyrone — (*There is an unsettled murmur from the clansmen*) — under the Great Seal of England — (*The murmur is louder*) and I will live as an English earl from this day out and I will extend this earldom over all the O'Neills. I have the support of the English and the colonists in this.

CLANSMAN 1 We're not used to the titles of the English here in Ulster.

O'NEILL You'll get used to them, O'Hagan.

CLANSMAN 2 They won't like this in Killetra and Brassilough.

O'NEILL They'll learn, O'Quinn. Times are changing. And we have to change too. We must live with the rest of the world.

CLANSMAN 1 Remember, Hugh O'Neill, the curse of your grandfather, Con Bacach, on all those who'd learn English, sow corn or build houses. It's against the nature of the Irish to do any of those things.

O'NEILL You're my fosterer, O'Hagan. I won't lie to you. Read the agreement, Cormac, which we've made with the English.

CORMAC (*Reads*) That the Earl of Tyrone shall now hold and control all the lands which he is able to hold or influence from his centre at Dungannon.

CLANSMAN 1 Aye, but what about your cousins? They won't

stand for any land-grabbing.

CLANSMAN 2 Aye, what about the sons of Shane O'Neill, your enemies with your own blood in their veins? They are out there somewhere in the rain, perishing like dogs, only waiting for you to turn your back and, cousins or not, they'll cut you to ribbons.

O'NEILL They are the breed of my father's murderer. They must be stamped out like vermin in the grass. They are the lice on my back and I'll not rest until I have them between finger and thumb. Go on back now to your cattle and your wives. In the summer there will be raids on our neighbours with plenty for the taking for everyone.

CLANSMAN 1 Arrah, Hugh, why did you ever have to bother with the English at all? Couldn't you be content as an O'Neill without all this business of earls? As The O'Neill you could rule Ulster unbeknownst to the English.

O'NEILL Why? Because this is how I've got whatever I have. I'm not a boy. I'm nearly forty. These have been long years. I can grow now like a spoilt pup because I'm fed from the hand of the master. I will have Ulster in time. But it can wait. It is now my interest and yours to bow and scrape before the English. Let me grow until I'm too big for Dungannon first. Then we can talk about Ulster.

The clansmen leave.

CORMAC There is more to it than that, surely?

ART Aye, begod. An English earl is more than fancy clothes and buckled shoes. The English don't hand out gifts like that without conditions on paper.

O'NEILL Yes. There is more to it than that.

CORMAC What is it, Hugh?

O'NEILL The English have decided to build one of their stone forts on the Blackwater.

CORMAC Ah God, that's the beginning of the end of us.

ART So and that's what ye went to Dublin for? The present of an English garrison? God Almighty give ye sense, man. Oh, Con Bacach was right. 'Tisn't the nature of the Irish to be hemmed in be buildings and walls. And that's only the first step. The English won't stop at that. Soon we'll have a sheriff, by God, with his judgement and his court. Well you mark me, Sir Earl. The O'Neills will have no garrison on their doorstep to peep at every one of their doings. The O'Neills will have no sheriff or gibbet or paper-written laws. It wasn't for this we ruled Ulster before Christ.

O'NEILL Oh have a bit of sense.

ART What? What? What's that ya said?

O'NEILL You heard what I said. This is the year 1587. You act as if it were the third century. Elizabeth is mistress of Ireland and the sea. The little we have we hold at her mercy.

ART Cowardly talk for the son of our father.

O'NEILL Besides there is much to be admired in the English. They are clean, civilized in dress. They can look beyond the limits of their own field. Can you? They are our masters in good order, government, and oneness in purpose. We can learn much from them.

ART I will not listen further or else I'll do damage.

Exit.

CORMAC He has reason, Hugh.

O'NEILL He is a fool! He has the hot blood of a bastard. The O'Neills will have no garrison on their doorstep! Did you ever! Who are the O'Neills, I ask you? An obscure declining family in the northwest corner of Europe trying to stand upright after centuries of sleep. God, how we Irish exaggerate our own importance!

CORMAC There is still fight in the people. They only need to be led.

O'NEILL Led? Look at their leaders. Cormac, you should have seen them in Dublin falling over one another to say a few words of ungrammatical English to the Lord Deputy. Trying to look comfortable in their

English britches. O'Donnell, Maguire, O'Rourke. It was a noble sight to see their faces washed. But as soon as they passed back from the towns they had forgotten the great, big civilized world and were back to their squabbles and their feuds and their cattle raids. For that is their nature, as brother Art would say.

CORMAC Then it is your nature too. For weren't you there in Dublin with them?

O'NEILL (*In anger*) If I was, I had no illusions about myself.

CORMAC Still and all, we cannot give way, Hugh. Haven't they installed Governors in Munster and Connaught? It'll be the turn of Ulster next.

O'NEILL By then we'll all be little English gentlemen or else buried with the rest of the O'Neills.

CORMAC How can you say such a thing?

O'NEILL I will not wear my family's past on my back like a bag. It will drag me down because it has the weight of the dead. Let the glorious past take care of itself.

CORMAC And you'll sit quiet and let every little pedlar and tinker come from England and take your land just like Mr Marshal Bagenal down below in Newry.

O'NEILL I spit the colonists out of my mouth.

CORMAC And that goes for the Bagenals too?

O'NEILL The Bagenals are the breed of a Newcastle tailor. They may give them titles but that is all colonials will ever be — tailors. They patch up the holes in the overcoat of the Empire.

CORMAC Rumour has it that you think otherwise.

O'NEILL (*Rising*) What do you mean by that?

CORMAC The people are talking of the way you're running after that one of the Bagenals. Mabel, is it?

O'NEILL Mabel. What are they saying?

CORMAC They're saying that it's wrong for the Irish to be mixing with those colonists.

O'NEILL They are, are they? Let them talk.

He walks downstage. He stands looking off in reverie.

(*Softly*) Mabel.

MAHON *and* O'FLANNIGAN *enter.*

MAHON (*To audience*) Sure come here will you. D'ya know who the fair lady is? Miss Mabel Bagenal no less, sister of the Marshal in Newry. That'll worry them in Dublin. An Irish chieftain hobnobbing with the daughter of an English colonist.

O'FLANNIGAN Is it true? Christ Almighty, the man must be mad, out of his mind with randiness.

MAHON They say the Marshal's in a dither. D'ya know what he roared at someone the other day — 'How would you like your sister to marry one of the wild Irish?'

O'FLANNIGAN He did, did he? Well God blast his black, ignorant, Protestant soul. The blood of the Irish is as good as the blood of the Anglo-Irish any day of the week. Still and all, O'Neill must have taken leave of his senses.

MAHON Yis and she only twenty and he nearly forty years of age. Isn't it awful? He-he!

O'FLANNIGAN Oh the dirty old man.

MAHON Yes, yes. Wouldn't you think now he'd be ashamed of himself running after a white slip of a girl like that —

MOYLE *enters quickly.*

MOYLE All of this must be taken down at once and reported to Dublin.

MAHON (*Eagerly*) Sir, I was just saying to your man here —

O'FLANNIGAN (*With a push*) Move over, there, ya little sparrowfart or I'll open ya! Well, Mr Moyle, sir. Can you credit it? O'Neill whoring with one of the Bagenals!

MOYLE It is news of the first importance. Fornication with a foreign woman may well diminish the affection which the native Irish have for O'Neill. They are sensitive on these matters if nothing else.

MAHON Ah, and they say, they say —

O'FLANNIGAN They say! They say! Get away outta that! Well, Mr Moyle, the Lord Deputy will pay well for this, hah?

MOYLE We must do our duty, Flannigan.

O'FLANNIGAN Oh, begod, yes, sir.

MOYLE Such rewards as we may gain are of secondary importance to the call of law and order.

O'FLANNIGAN Oh, aye sir, that's gospel —

> *They fade off in procession.* O'NEILL *is isolated in a spot.*

O'NEILL (*Whisper*) Mabel. Mabel.

> MABEL BAGENAL *comes running on. She steals up behind* O'NEILL *to startle him.*

MABEL (*Gruff voice*) I arrest you in the name of the Queen! Come quietly!

O'NEILL Mabel! Stop! Did anyone see you come here?

MABEL (*Happily counting*) Let's see. My father. Yes. My brother, the Marshal. The Provost Marshal. Then there was the Captain of the Guard — hundreds, really —

O'NEILL Stop it, you little fool. I'm serious.

MABEL So am I, as a matter of fact. Precisely who is it who frightens you? My brother? The Queen? Or just yourself?

O'NEILL Even you must not speak to me like that.

MABEL Oh dear!

O'NEILL You're so young —

MABEL I am a woman. I've loved you from the first moment I saw you.

O'NEILL You should hate me as the colonist hates the native.

MABEL I hate that word, colonist. Loyalist, maybe. But not colonist. It implies no rights.

O'NEILL (*Drily*) You are Irish. I am Irish. Madam, we are only separated by time, blood, religion. These are small things. History will not be able to tell the difference between us.

MABEL I should certainly hope not. If people have sense.

O'NEILL On the other hand you will never be Irish because you do not have the weight of time on your back.

MABEL Stop patronising me!

O'NEILL It's only an old man's game.

MABEL I happen to like older men, as a matter of fact. One
is never threatened, somehow. One is made to feel
secure.

O'NEILL My heart is old, Mabel, so old it feels like centuries.

MABEL Oh I think you have a loving, strong, brave heart.

O'NEILL Mabel, Mabel, you distract me from common sense.
What am I to do at all? Tell me —

MABEL Tell you what?

O'NEILL Tell me of when you first saw me.

MABEL I saw you first from my window in Newry riding
through the frosty streets one November. The
stones themselves were white with frost and
everything rang with a sound in the air. You were
on a roan mare and your beard was a flame under
your face. You wore a scarlet jacket with slashed
sleeves of yellow silk. There was a green cloak on
your back but it was thrown over to give you
freedom. A boy ran beside you, his hand on the
halter, and although his flesh was pink with the
cold, his eyes laughed. Above and around you was
the fog of breath from the three of you, yourself, the
boy, and the horse. The people all said you had
ridden from Dungannon with twenty pikemen
and a Spanish cleric and that the Marshal himself
could not restrain you even if he had the will to do
it.

O'NEILL You have a memory for many things, Lady Mabel.

MABEL Oh and I remember how, when the gates shut with
a great noise after you, I cried for hours.

O'NEILL Why did you cry? Oh why did you cry? Weren't
you much better off where you were?

MABEL I hated it. I hated it. You don't know what a garrison town can be like.

O'NEILL I can guess.

MABEL Oh how could you possibly — ? All those awful
wives sitting around all day worrying about Government pay and pensions, complaining about the
Irish servants and the Irish wars, boasting about
the time they were received by the Lord Deputy in

24

Dublin. I can't stand it much longer. Why can't they simply return to England? Quite obviously they hate Ireland.

O'NEILL Maybe they're being patriotic. To England, I mean. Spreading the glory of the Empire. Opening up new territory to civilization. That kind of thing.

MABEL Oh don't be sarcastic.

O'NEILL Madam, I couldn't be more serious. I have a great respect for English civilization, its good order and civil security, its sense of organization —

MABEL It can be awfully dull too —

O'NEILL We could do with a little dullness in Ireland nowadays.

MABEL Oh please don't say that. I think Ireland is terribly romantic. I look out over the town walls and I see forests and mists and mountains —

O'NEILL It rains interminably so that eventually your bones rot beneath your skin —

MABEL Is it true there are fairies and, oh, all kinds of things in the woods?

O'NEILL It is a convenient country to hide in —

MABEL I believe you Irish always picnic in the country without a table to eat from?

O'NEILL We eat off the ground, if that is what you mean. Indoors and out. It is a custom which brings man nearer to his fellow animal.

MABEL And the women —

O'NEILL What about the women?

MABEL They say that Irish women are very beautiful and that they've many lovers. (*In a whisper*) Hugh, how many wives have you had?

O'NEILL That's enough of that now.

MABEL But how many? Go on. Tell.

O'NEILL (*After a pause*) Three.

MABEL greets this with peals of laughter.

MABEL And how many children have you had?

O'NEILL I can't remember.

Their laughter together is cut short and they look at one another silently.

It's not true. I mean I remember them — all. It's only I've had so many daughters I've stopped counting. But I remember my son Owen, now.

MABEL Owen?

O'NEILL There was a boy! A wee devil. Wouldn't take orders from anyone. There was a spark of greatness in him.

MABEL Is he — dead?

O'NEILL (*Roughly*) Siobhán took him away with her when she went back to her own people.

MABEL Oh —

O'NEILL There. I knew you'd find our Ulster customs strange.

MABEL Oh but I don't! I think it's all absolutely wonderful. I'd give anything for such a life. I'd gather nuts and berries for my husband. I'd have him skin deer and dye pelts for our bed.

O'NEILL You haven't even begun to understand.

MABEL We'd eat wild honey and salmon and drink Spanish wine.

O'NEILL Spanish wine is not for loyalists like you and me, Mabel.

MABEL (*Near to tears*) Oh why are you always trying to depress me?

O'NEILL Because you're talking dream talk, girl. That's why. You haven't an earthly notion of what it's like to be in Dungannon.

MABEL But you said you'd welcome civility and good manners at Dungannon. I am not a particularly good housewife, Hugh, but I can learn. I'd give anything, anything to attend on you, to teach your womenfolk the comforts of living.

O'NEILL Huh! They'd quarter you within a week.

MABEL And who are *they*, might I ask?

O'NEILL They? They are the women of the clan. They are the hereditary whores of the O'Neills who carry daggers as other women carry pins.

MABEL I can take care of myself. And if I have to prove my love for you with a knife I can do that too.

O'NEILL I hadn't meant to frighten you, little robin. It's only that we're talking like the mad people.

MABEL Well let us be mad. It's about time you took something you really want, Hugh O'Neill. Oh Hugh, don't you want me?

O'NEILL Oh God, don't distract me. Want? The word is a weak one for what I feel. You are more like a sickness in me, Mabel. It is the fever which the famished get from eating green leaves off the trees.

MABEL And I want you, Hugh. What more is there to say?

O'NEILL Sometimes it is the cool white love that I have never been able to give one of my own daughters.

MABEL When you're away from me I think of you so often that we might as well be man and wife.

O'NEILL Sometimes I wish to savage your body like an animal which makes me afraid of my own thoughts.

MABEL (*Brightly, nervously*) Maybe then we can have a bishop for our wedding, Hugh?

O'NEILL Mabel, let us lie down together.

MABEL No, Hugh, no. (*Laughs nervously*) First you must smuggle me away across the Blackwater in your cloak. You remember how you used to promise? We'll elope.

O'NEILL Come here to me.

MABEL No, Hugh. I have to go now. (*Kisses him quickly and pirouettes away from his grasp*) I have to be off now before they come looking for me. *I — love — you.* And remember about the bishop.

Exit.

O'NEILL Elope! Bishop! God Almighty! (*Loudly*) Mabel! (*Quieter*) Mabel. (*Whisper*) Mabel.

Lights up. Downstage the waiting CORMAC *and* POET.

(*To* CORMAC) Yes, that is her name: Mabel. I am

	going to marry her, Cormac.
CORMAC	What? You must be mad, stark raving mad. Do you know what the clans are going to say to this? What reason is there in it, man?
O'NEILL	I have my reason.
CORMAC	Aye. The blind reason of a bull.
O'NEILL	I love her with a violence that is like constant anger. Besides she will bring civilized ways to Dungannon. We must take what is best from the new, modern world, Cormac.
CORMAC	Right. But remember, Hugh O'Neill, that your old world is far from dead.

He turns to go.

O'NEILL	Cormac. Send in a woman to me.
CORMAC	A woman. What woman?
O'NEILL	Any of the women that is handy outside. I have need of a woman.

Exit CORMAC.

	(*To* POET) Poet! Let us have entertainment. Sing the praises of the O'Neill. Sing that one about 'Conn, Son of Con, Son of Henry, Son of Owen, red-lipped ranger, most precious offspring of the Grecian Gael.'
POET	You mock me, Hugh O'Neill.
O'NEILL	No, no. Quite seriously, I enjoy the exaggeration. The excess.
POET	It is only the language of our poetry of praise. We only praise our own.
O'NEILL	I repeat. I enjoy it. Am I not Irish too?
POET	I will sing you something topical, Earl of Tyrone. It is a song of praise.
O'NEILL	More praises.
POET	Aye, in praise, mostly. (*Chants*) Man who apes the English ways, Who cut short your curling hair, You are unlike the son of Donncadh. Him I praise.

He would hate to have at his ankle a jewelled spur,
    stockings of the English.
Little he cares for gold-bordered cloaks.
The son of Donncadh, I praise.
He does not set his heart on a foreign bed,
He is content to lie upon rushes —

O'NEILL Poet, I could cut out your tongue.

POET It would be a poor remedy. A poet has no tongue.
He only shares the one tongue with many others.

O'NEILL I thought you said it was to be a poem of praise.

POET Give praise to one and you have to take something
from someone else.

O'NEILL Tell me, Poet, why it is you hate the clothes on my
back?

POET Three marks of the foreigner: gaudy clothes, a
strange language, and the desire to build houses.

O'NEILL But if it is for our better that we adopt strange
clothes and a strange language, what of that?

POET This is much bigger than you or I, Hugh O'Neill. It
is the nature of a people.

O'NEILL For God's sake, man, the Irish are no different from
any people on this earth.

POET It is the nature of the people. What was good for
your father and your father's father should be good
enough for you. You would sour the milk of your
mother and twist your bones into a new shape.

O'NEILL I would be a modern man, Poet, adding to myself
where I find something wanting, questioning myself
at all times for my own betterment.

POET You would trample on the traditions of your
people. You would have laws written on paper.

O'NEILL I will close my ears to no man.

POET Turn the river in its bed and you must call it by
another name!

O'NEILL Rhymer, we've nothing more to say to one another.
Get away from me. Out!

> As the POET exits, enter ROISIN. She is a black-
> haired, confident woman in her forties. She and the
> POET exchange looks of hostility.

O'NEILL (*Watching. With a laugh*) Hah! Competition!

ROISIN (*To* O'NEILL) There y'are, me fine cock. God forgive me, I'd begun to despair of you, Hugh O'Neill. I'd begun to wonder if the auld stir had died in you altogether and you with such a remarkable reputation to live up to with the women. Have you become stale with an overdose of wives?

> O'NEILL *reaches for her but she twirls out of his reach with a laugh.*

O'NEILL Come here to me.

ROISIN You'll have to catch me first.

O'NEILL Oh for Christ — (*Tiredly*) We're both beyond the stage of jumping around like goats. Let's get it over with.

ROISIN (*Pouting*) Is this what's due to me as a kept woman of the O'Neills?

O'NEILL Due! Due! What do you mean — due — you bitch! Does no one attend to me anymore in this cursed house? I'll lay the law down here.

ROISIN (*Rapid change. Seductively*) Hugh —

O'NEILL (*More subdued. Quietly*) I'm my own master. Whatever the ropes ye may have around my neck.

ROISIN Hugh, let us go and lie down —

O'NEILL Let us go and lie down. You know, I said much the same thing to her but she wouldn't have me.

ROISIN I know —

O'NEILL Elope! Bishop! A bishop! Elope — at my age!

ROISIN I know. I know.

O'NEILL (*Putting his hands on* ROISIN'S *face but looking over her head*) So young, so soft — (*Pulling himself together*) I'm afraid, Roisin, I don't have the inclination anymore.

ROISIN Hugh, there's nothing to hide from me, you know. I know well what you have for me isn't meant for me at all but for the wee girl. But sure isn't that what I'm here for, man? Now. Let you come back here with me and in the darkness — I'll let you see her face and not my face.

O'NEILL (*Touched*) Roisin. Am I still The O'Neill?

ROISIN Course y'are. What a question.

> *She goes upstage and reveals a pallet bed which she begins to arrange with cushions.*

O'NEILL I have nightmares, terrible nightmares. Figures torment me in my sleep. Figures of horsemen. They come galloping in silence out of the darkness, their mouths torn open for war screams. But — not a sound from them. Not a sound.

ROISIN You ought to be dreaming of your young honey girl and her white limbs.

O'NEILL With her I don't know where the hell I'm going.

ROISIN Come here to me. Come on. Tomorrow you can be thinking about that.

O'NEILL Am I to be the first of the Irish with an English britches and an English tongue? Or the last of the O'Neills? Answer me that. Or am I just something torn apart at the crotch between the two? What in God's name am I at all?

ROISIN (*Half kneeling on the bed. A low monotone*) You are Hugh, son of Ferdorcha, son of Con Bacach, son of Con, son of Henry, son of Owen —

> O'NEILL *looks towards her a moment and then walks slowly up to her. The lights fade. Drums and music.*
>
> *A sudden spot upon the* POET *who speaks out to the audience.*

POET (*Chanting*) Praise for the happy couple!
They are like two birds on the one bough,
Two blooms on the one stalk,
Two thoughts in the one head, before sleep,
Two rings on the one finger,
Two stones in the secret bed of the running stream.
Far and wide is the reputation of the new wife.
Mabel, mistress of Dungannon.
Each man leaves her table, heavy with hospitality.
Days pass unnoticed in her company.

In Dungannon the great door is closed.
In the house the women bind up their hair,
Young girls yawn and spin the thread,
And the cows grow heavy in the long grass.
Praise for the happy couple!
May they make men.

> *There is darkness for some minutes and music. Then lights up, on the forestage only at first.* O'NEILL *and* MABEL *enter from the right. She is on his arm but she appears to be tired and listless. The movement is very slow and when they halt there is a pause.*

MABEL (*Haltingly, listlessly*) Do I — do I have to go in?

O'NEILL Yes, you're my wife now.

MABEL You could say to them that I am — unwell.

O'NEILL Unwell? (*Coldly*) You are not unwell.

MABEL But you could say — you could pretend.

O'NEILL (*Impassively*) You are not unwell.

MABEL (*Holding her head*) Then it must be something worse than sickness.

O'NEILL (*Relentlessly*) You are not sick. There is nothing wrong with you. And what's more they'll know there's nothing wrong with you. Well? What am I supposed to do? Am I to tell them the truth? Am I to tell the clans that you don't want to sit and eat with them? Am I to tell my brothers that you despise their habits?

MABEL (*Weakly*) Oh, please.

O'NEILL Am I to tell my household that my wife considers herself superior to them? That their eating habits disgust her, that their smells make her wretch?

MABEL Oh Hugh, do my feelings not matter?

O'NEILL (*Explosively*) You are my wife. As such, woman, you must play my wife in front of the world. I am *The O'Neill*! Only half of myself belongs to myself — the other half belongs to the people.

MABEL (*Bitterly*) And half of me?

O'NEILL Mabel, Mabel, can't you at least do this much for me? What is it but to sit with the clans?

MABEL (*Stonily*) I'll do it for you.

O'NEILL (*In a false voice*) But sure it's going to be a fine banquet. Wait'll you see. The women have been working for weeks on it. And they've done their living best to follow your directions.

MABEL They have not.

O'NEILL How have they not?

MABEL They laughed at what I told them. And said the men would rise against my food.

O'NEILL (*Persisting*) It will be a great event and I want nothing to go wrong. Especially as Master Mountfort will be there.

MABEL (*Note of fear*) Mountfort?

O'NEILL Yes. The great English preacher —

MABEL I know who he is. You didn't tell me this. (*Fearfully*) Is he coming here?

O'NEILL He is here now this very minute.

MABEL (*Urgently*) Oh Hugh, what does all this mean? Does it mean that you are going to fight?

O'NEILL (*Moving away, evasively*) Why? Would you report me to your brother, the Marshal?

MABEL That is unworthy of our love.

O'NEILL I am sorry.

MABEL Oh God, what has happened to us that we cannot seem to talk to one another any more.

Pause.

I am afraid.

O'NEILL I said I was sorry, didn't I? The arrival of Mountfort means — nothing.

MABEL I'm not afraid of Mountfort and his Holy War. I am afraid of you.

O'NEILL Of me?

MABEL Yes, you.

O'NEILL (*With a nervous laugh*) Hah! I told you. It means nothing to me. Priest or Queen. I wash my hands of them.

MABEL (*Fiercely*) Hugh, that is what terrifies me. What kind of a man are you that you cannot give yourself to the one thing, ever.

O'NEILL I give myself — I give myself entirely — to you.

MABEL No, you don't. I'm only your pretty little robin. (*Bitterly*) I'm your showpiece. You believe yourself too wise, too smart, to lay yourself at the feet of any one person or any one cause, whether it's loving or fighting. But that's no wisdom. It's only a kind of weakness inside you —

O'NEILL (*Blustering*) You wrong me. I can't — a man in my position can't be too careful.

MABEL (*With conviction*) Hugh, drive out this priest. Send him away. Then we can build our house together.

O'NEILL I can't do that and you know it.

MABEL (*Beyond control*) Then fight; do the opposite.

O'NEILL What?

MABEL Go and give yourself to Mountfort and his Holy War.

O'NEILL That's strange kind of talk from you.

MABEL I hate the very thought of war. I hate its suffering. I hate this priest and all that he stands for. But I'd have you do one thing or the other. Then there'd be one meaning to you. I'd know you then as a man. You're one thing to one man and something else to another. It's like being a living lie.

O'NEILL It's my — blood —

MABEL It's you, you!

O'NEILL Woman, it's my race. Don't you see I'm trying to rise above the petty mind of those around me. If I'm splintered it's because my people have eyes only for their own bits of property. Good God, I'm struggling with generations of small-minded men. And I'm the only one who sees this, the only one —

MABEL Then fight, fight —

O'NEILL I do not choose — to fight —

MABEL Well, tell the men you are loyal then —

O'NEILL (*Indulgently*) Mabel, Mabel. You must leave matters of politics to me. They're beyond the understanding of a woman.

MABEL We're not talking about politics. (*Tiredly*) We're talking about you if you would simply see it.

O'NEILL (*Fiercely*) I can't make mistakes — A man like me

can't afford to make mistakes.

MABEL We must make mistakes before doing right. Don't you know that?

O'NEILL (*Slowly*) A mistake by me could cut the country open from top to bottom. Not just Dungannon and Tyrone but Tyrconnell and Tyrrell and all that remains.

MABEL We'd be still left together, Hugh —

O'NEILL (*Gently*) Indeed, and you're no longer the little robin now.

MABEL No, Hugh. I'm no longer a child.

O'NEILL Maybe I was born in the wrong place and at the wrong time. Maybe I'm the wrong man. Hm? The Italian says it's better for a prince to be feared than to be loved. I cannot learn that lesson fully. I've come a long way without having to give myself fully to the sword metal in my hand.

MABEL Oh, I do love you, Hugh O'Neill, despite the heartache that you cause me. You're a strange, cautious man.

Pause.

But I cannot stick this life much longer if you refuse to face yourself!

O'NEILL Come, Mabel, can't we go in to the banquet now?

MABEL Wait. There's the woman. What will you do with the woman?

O'NEILL Which woman?

MABEL That foul, dirty creature that's in the house. When are you going to put her out?

O'NEILL Roisin, is it? Is it Roisin, you mean?

MABEL You know who I mean. We've talked about it only yesterday. You said —

O'NEILL (*Testily*) I said she was part of the household, was so in the past, and would have to be so in the future. Can't we go in now?

MABEL Hugh, you don't even listen to what I say. I cannot live under the same roof as that — that living insult to me.

O'NEILL	We'll talk about it tomorrow.
MABEL	You're not heeding what I said.
O'NEILL	(*Finally*) We have to go in to the banquet now. They'll be expecting us.
MABEL	Do I really have to — go? I mean — do I have to? I could come later perhaps?
O'NEILL	No.
MABEL	Can you not say — say I am unwell.
O'NEILL	But you are not unwell. And what would they say of me? Of us? You are my wife.
MABEL	Well, I'll go then. Because I am your wife.
O'NEILL	But you'll find it interesting. This Master Mountfort now —

> O'NEILL *continues whispering to her as they walk centre downstage. Gradually lights up on the Banquet Hall of Dungannon Castle. Master* MOUNTFORT *stands to one side with his clerics who carry the banner* SPES NOSTRA JESU ET MARIA. *There stands, also, the* POET. CORMAC, ART *and* CLANSMEN *stand uneasily around the table, centre. This table is simply a rough platform, a couple of inches off the floor. Spits, flagons and cauldrons are displayed and there is a movement of servants. All sit, when they are seated, on piled rushes.* O'NEILL *and* MABEL *take their places, standing, at the very centre of the group by the table.*

(*With a gesture*) You may begin now, Master Mountfort.

MOUNTFORT What I have to say can be soon said. Men of Ireland, the hour is late. The rest of Europe is already on the march. We have carried this banner now to Ulster from a great distance. And now, out of the North, will come vengeance. Let the dragon of Fitzmaurice be replaced on this banner by the Red Hand of Ulster. Let us call on the clans to unite, to stand shoulder to shoulder for Ireland, for the Faith —

*The clansmen cough and shuffle as at the end of a
sermon.*

O'NEILL Will you not come and sit with us, Father Mountfort?

MOUNTFORT We will stand, Hugh O'Neill, until you've finished.

O'NEILL *and the others sit. The clansmen settle
themselves heavily and resume drinking. A lull.*

CLANSMAN 1 They say all Connaught is black in ashes.

CLANSMAN 2 Aye. And that the smell of burning is floating
across the Erne into Ulster.

CLANSMAN 1 The English will have us destroyed yet.

CLANSMAN 2 They say this Captain Willis is a terror.

CLANSMAN 1 A red divil! He scoured through Maguire's territory, sweeping every creature out of the bowels of
the land.

CLANSMAN 2 Maguire is finished so, if the English have turned
their eyes on him.

ART Can't ye see, can't ye, what it's all leading to? That
we're next? Let Maguire fall, and there's nothing
between us and the English. 'Twon't do us much
good then to keep house with an English wife, I'm
telling you.

CORMAC That will do you now, Art.

O'NEILL Let him be, Cormac. He doesn't understand.

ART Ah — He doesn't understand, doesn't he. Maybe
he doesn't know how to go arse-licking with his
colonist friends. Well bejaysus here's one O'Neill
who won't go running cap-in-hand for a pardon
every time the wind blows hard from Dublin.

O'NEILL *(Wearily)* I've told you a thousand times we're not
ready. You fool. We have to play for time, pretend
our loyalty —

ART That's not what you said yesterday.

O'NEILL What did I say yesterday?

ART That we'd be the greatest earldom of the empire,
equal to the English nobility.

O'NEILL That might have been true yesterday.

ART And tomorrow you'll have a different story, no doubt.

O'NEILL There's no tomorrow, brother Art. Only today and it's hard enough keeping track of that.

Enter ROISIN.

ROISIN God save us all from harm but will you look at the sheep's eyes and the long faces. What's come over us at all? We're turning Dungannon into a monastery, saving your reverend's presence.

There is a general uproar from the men who shout encouragement and obscenities at her.

(*Ignoring all but* O'NEILL *and* MABEL) It wasn't like that when Siobhán was wife to Hugh, I'm telling you. A man could spit then where he wanted to without being told he was no gentleman.

O'NEILL (*Dully*) Put that woman out.

ROISIN (*Escaping the lurch of a clansman*) There was a time when you'd have wanted your kept woman beside you, Hugh O'Neill, after your dinner with your belly full and the old urge rising in you. But you've become so good-living now, surrounded be the clergy and under the eye of an educated wife.

MABEL (*In a light voice*) Will no one put that foul woman out?

ROISIN Aha. The chicken has a tongue. Foul, she says, the parched little creature. Let her know who she is talking to. Tell her that I and my mother and my mother's mother have served the bed of the O'Neills before her breed had a name. Tell her that we had the ear of princes while her likes peddled rags on the streets of an English town.

MABEL (*Frantically to* O'NEILL) Will you stop this dirty person from insulting me?

O'NEILL Pay no attention to her, can't you?

ROISIN (*To* MABEL) I've me rights here too that no sugar face is going to whip away from me.

MABEL   (*Rising, slowly. To* O'NEILL) Will you sit silent while
         your wife is spoken to like that?
O'NEILL   (*To* MABEL) Sit down, sit down, can't you.
MABEL   Have you not heard what I said?
O'NEILL   It's of no consequence, it's of no consequence.
MABEL   Oh, it is of great consequence!
O'NEILL   (*In a fierce whisper*) Stop driving me beyond myself.
MABEL   Put her out, put her out. Either she goes or I go.
O'NEILL   What kind of carry-on is this in front of everyone?
         D'you see the disgrace you're making of yourself?
MABEL   Make up your mind, make up your mind.
ROISIN   (*Confident now. To* CLANSMEN) Will ye come here a
         minute until I tell yes what a little birdie told me? A
         certain party — no names mentioned now — hasn't
         found marriage all a bed of roses. It was all lovey-
         duckey the first week or so but sure you can't keep
         a tired horse on the road forever —
O'NEILL   (*As* MABEL *cries out. To* ROISIN) Get out. That's no
         way to be talking in front of the priest.
ROISIN   It's a change for you to be worried about priests.
         There was a time when the flood of manhood was
         on you and there was no power in Heaven and Earth
         that'd interrupt your purpose. But you're tired
         now, Hugh O'Neill, and fit company for a wee girl.
MABEL   How dare you! How —

         O'NEILL *signals to attendants who come forward to*
         ROISIN *but she shoves them off.*

ROISIN   I'll go myself if that's what's wanted of me. (*Goes to*
         MABEL) You'll rue the day you came into this house.
MABEL   (*Simply*) I'm not afraid of you. You're a foul woman.
         I'm not afraid of you. I'm simply afraid of the
         power that will allow you to stand there free to
         insult me. And that terrifies me, that darkness, that
         blackness. (*To* O'NEILL. *To the men*) Why cannot any
         of you speak out?

         ROISIN *makes a sign with her hands on the floor and
         spits.*

ROISIN   The curse of the barren on you, new woman. May
         your belly wither to the size of a nut, may your tits
         dry up in you. May the flesh fall from you in a
         sweat —

O'NEILL   Out! Out! (ROISIN *backs away, still mumbling*) Now,
          now can we have a little peace.

MABEL   (*Calmly*) Do you have nothing more to say but that?

O'NEILL   Silence, woman. Hasn't there been enough of this?
          I won't have woman-fights in front of our guests,
          in front of the clans.

MABEL   (*Staggering to the centre of the room*) I won't stand
         this any longer, I'm telling you — I'm not going to.
         I won't. I won't.

CLANSMAN 1   What the hell's come over her now?

MABEL   (*Hysterically*) Oh I can only laugh, laugh at all your
         grand talk. (*With wild gestures*) Countess of Tyrone.
         My noble palace. My courtiers. My jester. Oh God,
         what dark place have I stepped back into out of the
         daylight?

O'NEILL   Mabel! Mabel!

MABEL   Don't you dare. Don't you dare talk to me, you. I've
         had enough of your soft talk.

CLANSMAN 1   Aye, she needs taming and putting in her place,
             that one.

MABEL   Listen to them! That is their notion of behaviour
         before a lady with their crude language and dirty
         habits.

O'NEILL   You're easily upset.

MABEL   Yes, I'm upset. I have my dignity. I know what is
         right and what is wrong.

O'NEILL   You learned that from your brother and your
          father, I suppose.

MABEL   Yes, I learned it from my father and my brother. At
         least they were gentlemen.

O'NEILL   Gentlemen!

MABEL   Yes, gentlemen, and for all your boasting of your
         noble blood you are not that yet.

ART   That's the way she's been going on since the first
         day she came here. Running down the Irish at
         every opportunity. Telling us how to clean our

noses, how to dress ourselves, where to piss. God
Almighty, you'd want patience to put up with it.

MABEL There is little hope of changing your ways. That's
another lesson I've learned to my cost. (*To* O'NEILL)
I tried. I tried to make you a civil home but they
only laughed at me and called me names. Oh where
are all the dreams we once had, Hugh? The hopes?

ART And what call had you coming here thinking to
change us? We have our ways, our laws, and our
language, the same as the English have, and we're
proud of them. If you can't put up with us, can't
you leave us be?

MABEL (*To* O'NEILL) Will you sit there silent? Must you
have this fellow answer for you?

O'NEILL His answer is as good as my answer. Isn't he my
brother?

MABEL Oh that's so typical of you. God, it's so typical of
you. Why don't you come out into the open and say
what you mean?

ART What kind of talk is that? Hugh, will you have her
run down your own brother now?

MABEL What do I care about his brothers? I love a man not
his family. What do I care about his cousins, his
uncles, his clans? Oh, I'm sick to death of the name
O'Neill. You're all so proud of yourselves, aren't
you? But you'll kill one another just as quickly as
you're ready to love.

O'NEILL That's enough out of you now.

MABEL (*Shrilly*) What happened to Phelim Mac Turlach
O'Neill? Wasn't he an O'Neill too or only a cousin
who had to die?

O'NEILL (*Loudly*) Silence, you silly woman.

MABEL Yes. I stood with you and your henchmen while
they cut him down. I can see him still, a great
bleeding hulk. They chopped at him until his arms
fell from his shoulders like lumps of leather. And
his son, Donal Óg. His son they drowned like a pup
in the river Bann while we stood by. I can hear his
small voice still coming up out of the water.

She weeps. There is a terrible silence and the
CLANSMEN *rise in their seats.*

O'NEILL (*With a great voice*) Don't question us, woman.
What can you know of this? We have our law which
was our law before Christ's law.

MABEL (*With a great sob*) You've named yourself with your
own words.

O'NEILL Mabel, Mabel, you do not understand.

MABEL I understand that you are not the man I loved.

O'NEILL I am the same man.

MABEL No, Hugh. The man I loved was not a prisoner. He
was going to throw off the chains of a dead past
from his people.

O'NEILL We will talk of this in private.

MABEL No, Hugh. It's about time you looked at yourself in
public. Can you not see that it's going to drag you
down? The savagery, the fear of everything that
isn't Irish. Oh, Hugh, this place might as well be
your tomb.

O'NEILL You can never know what it is to be O'Neill. Maybe
soon no one will know because these days are
impatient for change. They create nobility now in a
day when it once took centuries. (*In a rising voice*)
Take away my name and I am a nobody. Don't
torment me, woman. If this place is to be my tomb,
then I was measured for it.

MABEL Alright, Hugh. Alright.

She rushes off in tears.

ART Let her be off outta that, back to her brother, the
Marshal. You should never have had any truck
with her at all in the first place.

CLANSMAN 1 She's not one of us, Hugh. She was lost amongst us.

CLANSMAN 2 Their ways are not our ways. The English blood
makes them English always.

ART More reason why we should go and burn to the
ground that blasted fort the English have down
there on the Blackwater.

CORMAC She's young, Hugh. She will over it in next to no time.

O'NEILL No, Cormac, she's no longer a girl. Didn't you see her grow with her pain? It's sad to be part of it.

CORMAC You musn't go blaming yourself for it.

O'NEILL It is the deception, Cormac, the deception. The old, tired prick which makes us forget our age and sense. I wish she were my daughter now instead of my wife.

CORMAC You were right to speak as you did.

O'NEILL Right? Wrong? I have little enthusiasm for words like those now, Cormac. She really believed me, Cormac. She threw away her life at my grand words. How much of it all was the truth, I wonder? How much did I really believe in the polish of an English accent, the cut of an English coat?

MOUNTFORT My lord O'Neill, I must speak to you.

O'NEILL Master Mountfort, I've heard that you've had great success among the people. Do you think it right to preach rebellion to a people that are at peace?

MOUNTFORT I've noticed that your people are the best armed and the best trained in the country.

O'NEILL (*With a chuckle*) You're a dangerous guest, Master Mountfort.

MOUNTFORT What I cannot understand is why you haven't moved before now when the English were on their knees.

O'NEILL Oh, priest, don't you start with that. I'd have moved long ago if I could have depended on my people.

ART Give us your blessing, Father, and be the Holy Trinity we'll burn everything English between here and Dublin.

O'NEILL How do you make someone like that see that his war is being fought too in the mouth of Tagus? What does he care what happened at Zutphen or Corunna? As long as he can clout his neighbour and steal a few cattle he's happy. England is only a bigger target to him than his neighbour over the hill. How do you begin, Master Mountfort? How do you begin to make a small island part of Europe when it has been isolated for so long on the white edge of the ocean? I'm beginning to think the whore is right just now. I am tired. I am old. Do you know I'm nearly forty-three?

MOUNTFORT It is the proper age of leadership.

O'NEILL I tell myself again and again that this old Gaelic world is dead. All that old rhymer carries there in his head is material now only for libraries. Our future, Master Mountfort, what of our future?

MOUNTFORT I think it is as clear as if the Almighty had leaned down to speak in your ear.

O'NEILL What do you mean, it's clear?

MOUNTFORT My lord, let us not waste words. In this century the great orb of Christendom has been broken and must be repaired. Unless we succeed in drawing all back to Rome the generations to come will see great divisions in Christianity. Lord O'Neill, we are in a great movement of unity, unity of state and faith, where Pope and Prince may encompass our total existence. We are trying to establish the fixed poles of our universe, Church and State. This is harmony, order and the true end of politics.

O'NEILL I'm afraid, Master Mountfort, our people too are split. They are seldom one on anything.

MOUNTFORT It is our mission to make them one, Lord O'Neill. (*Quite carried away*) Brother and brother, clan and clan, colonist and native, all in Ireland must melt into a common purpose, tempered with this one, white, cold flame of true faith. This is the forge for your sword, Hugh O'Neill.

ART Arrah Master Mountfort, you're an Englishman. You wouldn't understand the people over here. Sure we'll be able to settle everything ourselves, won't we, lads?

CLANSMEN Begod, we will. Aye, we can.

ART We'll go out now and show the Protestants how to fight, so we will. And with the help of God and our own St Patrick and St Brigid we'll drive the buggers into the Irish say (*sea*).

O'NEILL (*With a roar of laughter*) There's your ally, Master Mountfort. Mother Church and Mother Ireland. Your great European dream becomes a local matter when it is transplanted in Ireland.

MOUNTFORT (*The intensity of his words captures everyone*) I am here to preach war, not peace. It is the hour of the eagle, not the dove. We — the priests of God — are compelled to stand in the wilderness while the heretic stables his horses in our churches.

CLANSMEN Ah, wouldn't we be better off to lave religion out of it altogether.

There are murmurs of agreement.

MOUNTFORT Beware, beware, I say. There will be those among you, I know, who will tell you that it is not the business of the priest to preach politics. Let him stick to his prayers, I hear them say. This I can tell you is the most pernicious doctrine of the day.

Pauses for effect.

Such self-styled theologians will tell you that it is your God-given duty to obey your lawful monarch. They will say that from the seat of the Government flows the order of society, justice, decorum and the rule of law. This in itself is true. But listen to me, men of Ireland. We are not here dealing with our lawful Prince. We are confronted with the usurper, Elizabeth. This she-serpent, Elizabeth, put out the light of Christendom. Satan now reigns in the guise of a female. This Jezabel has come out of darkness, armed, and must be cut down with the sword of righteousness.

He produces a scroll.

In the very words of His Holiness Pope Pius V in the sacred bull, *Regnans in Excelsis*, it is proclaimed that Elizabeth is deposed from her throne and cast out in excommunication from the One, True, and Roman Church, and that her subjects are thereby relieved of all allegiance. Given under the seal of the Fisherman, fifteen hundred and seventy.

I say to you that when a government seeks to undermine our Faith it is a grave, moral duty on all of us to take up arms against that government. Christians of Ireland, that is your crusade and this (*taking the banner*) is your standard. Look at it. It has already been stained by the blood of martyrs. It was carried by Fitzmaurice in the Holy War of Munster. When the tyrant Elizabeth caused the men of Munster to die in torture she left us this relic lest we forget, and we will not forget. Our prayer must be the prayer of valorous Judith in the Bible who would not allow the foreigner, the unbeliever, to ravish her. In this way too we pray as the raging enemy seeks to lay hands on the fair limbs of our virgin land. 'Lift up Thy arms as from the beginning, O Lord, and crush their power with Thy power. Let their power fall with Thy wrath who promise themselves to violate Thy sanctuary and defile the dwelling place of Thy Name and to beat down with their sword the horn of Thy Altar.'

CLERICS Amen.

There is a pause. Sudden outcry off. GILLABOY O'FLANNIGAN *comes racing in breathlessly.*

O'FLANNIGAN God be with you, O'Neill.

O'NEILL May you choke on your own words, spy.

O'FLANNIGAN Ah, Jaysus, that's no way to talk to an innocent man and he having news for you.

O'NEILL How much will it cost me, O'Flannigan?

O'FLANNIGAN Ah now, sir, is that fair? I ask you. Is it now? Honest to Christ I've given up the English.

O'NEILL Out with it.

O'FLANNIGAN The English are preparing the biggest army yet to invade Tyrone. Aye. They tell in Newry of how the Marshal Bagenal himself will lead the five thousand men into Tyrone to revenge the whoring of his sister.

O'NEILL She was willing at the time. Go back and tell him that.

CORMAC What do we do now, Hugh?

O'NEILL Prepare for war. Not just raids, Cormac, but war, total war.

MOUNTFORT Kneel, men of Ireland. For the Pope and for Ireland!

All kneel except O'FLANNIGAN, O'NEILL, *and* CORMAC.

CORMAC Is this what you want, Hugh, this Holy War?

O'NEILL It's what we have to take whether we like it or not. I've been waiting for Bagenal to move. Religion may be just what we need now, Cormac. The cement — so let's have prayers.

O'FLANNIGAN There's still more, Hugh O'Neill.

O'NEILL More?

O'FLANNIGAN Aye. (*Nervously*) I meself just passed the Countess Mabel a while back riding away towards Newry.

O'NEILL Mabel. Poor little robin. Let the Marshal Bagenal come, O'Flannigan. We'll welcome him. He now has back in Newry the one pledge of his safety! (*To* CORMAC) You know, Cormac, she wanted me to rebel, the girl. Would you believe it? She thought it'd help to straighten out the crooked passages of my old heart. (*He chuckles*) So let's give ourselves to this Holy War —

O'NEILL, CORMAC, *and* O'FLANNIGAN *kneel.*

MOUNTFORT To the restoration of Catholic Ireland as it was before this present darkness we humbly dedicate these arms, this standard for the greater glory of the Father, the Son, and the Holy Ghost.

EXSURGE, DOMINE, ADJURA NOS ET LIBERA NOS.

Music and fade-out.

ACT TWO

Exactly as in Act One. Before the rise of the curtain there is the rumble of battle, occasional gunfire, the shrillness of war-pipes, the scream of war-cries. The curtain rises on a crowded stage. Across the backcloth drifts the black smoke of pillage. There is the suggestion of great, distant fires. Corpses hang from poles roundabout. Upstage, on platforms, a tent-like structure. Pikes stand upright beside it. To the side, also upright, is the standard of Fitzmaurice: SPES NOSTRA, JESU ET MARIA. *Other colours and weapons are on display.*

The Yellow Ford. A great battle has just been fought. For some moments there is great movement. O'NEILL *stands centre, surrounded by* ART, CORMAC, *and* CLANSMEN. *The men are drained of all energy, only supported by the fierce exultation of butchery and success. Master* MOUNTFORT *occupies a prominent position.*

The drums beat.

O'NEILL   Read out your claims now, Master Mountfort, so that everyone may know what Ireland demands.

MOUNTFORT   The claims of O'Neill, Prince of Ulster, given out at the Yellow Ford in the heat of this great victory over the English:

> One: That the Catholic, Apostolic and Roman religion be openly preached and taught throughout Ireland as it was in times past.
>
> Two: That there be erected a university upon the crown rents of Ireland, wherein all sciences shall be taught according to the manner of the Roman Catholic Church.
>
> Three: That O'Neill and O'Donnell with all their partakers may peaceably enjoy all lands and privileges that did appertain to their predecessors, two hundred years ago.

Enter CECIL *and* MOUNTJOY *downstage.*

CECIL   (*Excitedly*) Stop! Stop! This can't go on. Utopia! Utopia! (*To* MOUNTJOY) This fellow O'Neill really means to be head and monarch of all Ireland. (*Waves a document*) Listen further to this: (*Reads*) Four: That all statutes made against the preferment of Irishmen be rescinded.

Absolute treason, my lord!

MOUNTJOY   Oh, it was to be expected, I mean you get this type of thing at the climax of all rebellions.

> *The following is played out against the silent assembly of* O'NEILL *and his group.*

CECIL   You are cool, for someone who has just been appointed Lord Deputy of Ireland.

MOUNTJOY   I am honoured by the responsibility.

CECIL   I do not have to tell you that it is a time of great crisis for the safety of the realm.

MOUNTJOY   We are prepared.

CECIL   (*Waves papers*) I've also some reports here of how the natives have responded to O'Neill's proclamation.

MOUNTJOY   You don't need to read them to me. I know already what's in them. The people are in revolt! The people are in the streets shouting their support of the Great O'Neill!

CECIL   Exactly! From all over the country. Each day brings us fresh rumour of a demonstration of popular zeal.

MOUNTJOY   Really! Do we have to give heed to such nonsense? I mean, tomorrow, when the wind is from another direction the mob will simply melt away.

CECIL   Let us see — let us see —

> CECIL *and* MOUNTJOY *compose themselves to observe and listen to the three spies who now enter. The three come forward as far as possible and speak to the audience directly. The O'Neill group is still impassive in the background.*

MOYLE I'm sure I'm speaking on behalf of all here present when I say how happy we are, I might say, how proud we all are at the success of the great Earl of Tyrone over the past five or six years in his war against the English. He is, I might say, a fine Irishman, a credit to his country. Of course the O'Neills are fine stock. Related to them myself, as a matter of fact, on the wife's side.

O'FLANNIGAN Listen here. I've fought with O'Neill and O'Donnell. I was with Cormac O'Neill at the Ford of the Biscuits in '94. I did me share of damage. (*He takes out a bottle and takes a nip*) Bejaysus, if there's anyone here that says I'm not a good Irishman I'll make hames of them.

MAHON They're hard times, God help us. O'Neill is master of all Ulster. You couldn't put your nose outside Newry without his permission. What if I do sell to the Irish and English on the same day? I'm a merchant, amn't I? I have to watch me business.

MOYLE I've always put my country first. That's why I'm in politics, you know. It's difficult when you're a county official as I am. You have to be careful who you give your support to. People look up to you, you know, in the district. Of course it isn't often that the country produces someone like O'Neill. Look at the way in which he has kept the English at bay for the past six years.

O'FLANNIGAN I was at Clontibret, boy, the day O'Neill cut the feathers off Bagenal. I — I was in the thick of it meself. Boy, I'm telling you I made bits of many an Englishman that day. (*Drinks from his bottle*)

MAHON It's hard to know who's up and who's down. One day it's the Irish, the next day it's the English. It's the poor people like us that suffers at the end of it all.

MOYLE It's the good of the country only that I'm thinking of.

O'FLANNIGAN Down with the whore Elizabeth.

MAHON We have to make a living, haven't we?

MOYLE I'm Irish. I may be one of the higher classes, but I

still have an Irish heart in my body like us all.

O'FLANNIGAN I'm Irish. I'd open anyone who'd say otherwise.

MAHON I'm a shopkeeper. Does it matter where I'm from? Isn't business the same everywhere?

MOYLE The point is that duty calls. I and my — ah — colleagues are putting our experience at the service of the new Ireland.

O'FLANNIGAN Look at me arm I damaged fighting for Ireland on the Erne. What more proof do ye need?

MOYLE Quite, quite. As I was saying, I have always been ready to serve my country. It's always best to give the experienced man the job. I know this well from my own local appointments. We must be fully prepared to join in the new Europe.

O'FLANNIGAN I don't give a twopenny curse who we're fighting. Europe be damned! Just give me a sword, boy, that's all.

MAHON What will all this have to do with the small businessman? That's what I'd like to know. We'd be far better off having little to do with these Spaniards. Next minute they'll be coming over here taking over our shops, undercutting our prices. We wouldn't be able to keep up with competition like that. (*To* O'FLANNIGAN) Do ya think we oughta secure our own interests be keeping in with the English? After all, O'Neill mightn't last long.

O'FLANNIGAN What's that? Haven't we the best fighting men in the world?

MAHON They say it costs him five hundred pounds a day to keep going. He can't stand that for long more.

O'FLANNIGAN What? What? Are you sure? Maybe — Hey, Mr Moyle, sir. (*He confers silently with* MOYLE)

MOYLE Hm, yes, I see —

The three begin to talk excitedly among themselves as they fade off together into the shadows.

MOUNTJOY I think we may dispense with the rumours of a popular uprising among the natives, my lord.

CECIL   I see what you mean.

MOUNTJOY It has been a strange study. Such a small island and
          so divided. I don't believe that O'Neill has the
          persuasion to unity available to him. He has a
          mangled history to contend with.

CECIL   Well, then! Let's go over the details of your
          supplies once more.

MOUNTJOY Not again?

CECIL   We can't be too diligent. Everything has to be clear.
          You said so yourself.

MOUNTJOY Everything is perfectly clear.

CECIL   Just once more now.

MOUNTJOY Oh, very well.

> *They seat themselves at a table to the side of the
> apron before a large pile of papers and then they are
> blacked out.*

O'NEILL   (*Coming alive among his men*) We are fighting for a
          new Europe. Unity of all in the Mystical Body of
          Christ. Ireland will be part of a new confederation
          as an independent member. We must all prepare
          ourselves. There is so little time. The ruins of our
          antiquity must be rebuilt on new foundations.
          New foundations —

> *He pauses and puts his head in his hands.*

ART   It worked! It worked as you said it would, Hugh,
          me boy. We rushed in and out like flies off a cow's
          back. And they got slower and slower so that we
          picked them off like fruit. Oh ho! The way we
          rushed the buggers when they ran out of powder.

CORMAC   Are you not well, Hugh?

O'NEILL   I'm well enough, Cormac. How do we stand now?

CORMAC   The men are stealing from the dead. O'Donnell is
          leading cavalry after the English who are gone into
          Armagh. There are thousands of the English dead
          out there, Hugh.

ART   Aye, and our friend Bagenal amongst them. He

won't pester the O'Neills again.

O'NEILL Poor Mabel. Poor little robin. Tell the men to take nothing from the dead but weapons.

CORMAC You know, Hugh, that before daybreak the women and children of the area will have swept even the clothes from the bodies. Isn't it better for the men to have what they can get?

ART And what is their right too, by custom.

O'NEILL Custom! Custom! Go do as I say and have the men form into their regiments in good order. Have every clansman prepare a list of the living. There is something growing around us, Cormac. I can feel it in the air.

CORMAC The men are swelled up with the victory, Hugh. They were shouting a while back that the Pope had a crown ready for you.

O'NEILL I could feel it as I looked out over that littered, broken road today and the steaming, raw heaps of the dead. It was like the cutting of a great abscess across the face of the land. It is war, Cormac. However just our cause may be we use the same sword, open the same wounds, release the same poison as the other fellow. Look at the men. They're crazed. Yelling anything that is in their heads without sense to it. I will never be the same again, Cormac, after this day.

CORMAC Oh Hugh, what sort of talk is that when you've become the liberator of your people, the Messiah?

O'NEILL I have become no such thing, Cormac. I'm not at all sure that our people want a Messiah. But whatever they want I am their servant now as surely as if I were paid a wage. I can only serve them now, in the way I know best.

ART We're ready now to move against the Blackwater fort.

O'NEILL Tomorrow, tomorrow.

ART Tomorrow there is Armagh. Then Newry. Then Dublin.

O'NEILL You're an impatient man, brother Art.

ART You see them corpses? I won't rest until everything

on two feet below in that fort is swinging like that. I won't be aisy until every English eyesore is gone off the face of Ulster.

O'NEILL I've arranged terms with the fort.

ART You've what?

O'NEILL It has surrendered. Its garrison will march away in safety, leaving colours, drums and ammunition behind them.

ART Jaysus, what a loss. Come on and we'll catch the remains of Bagenal's army before it gets to Armagh.

O'NEILL I've also arranged terms with it. It will march for Dublin in a few days with its full colours.

ART Hah? And I suppose you'll be bowing to the Council in Dublin next? After the greatest victory against the English since they set foot in the country!

O'NEILL I will arrange pardon if I can.

ART Never. Begod we've done enough like that. D'ya want every dacent Irishman in the country to be laughing at us?

O'NEILL (*Tiredly*) You are a poor sort of fool, brother Art. And it is fools like you that have us the way we are. Now you listen to what will be done because I, The O'Neill, have decided so. We can't take another step without Spanish help. And it hasn't arrived yet. So let there be no more talk about honour and glory. We may get where we want to go with a quiet courage and if each man meets his destiny with dignity and a belief in his own worth. It is not bravado we want, brother Art, but self-respect.

Lights low. To the men.

Light fires across the hill tops. Let the English know before sleep that we are out here, armed. Watchful. And let us watch for the enemies within us that are greater by far than all the machinery of war of the great Elizabeth —

54

Drums. Fade out.

Lights up forestage on CECIL *and* MOUNTJOY *busy with their papers. Hold the pause a moment.*

MOUNTJOY Yes, yes. I see that. Now what else is there?

CECIL (*Busily*) You take this proclamation. And here are details of your 12,000 foot, 1,200 horse. This here is our contract with the merchants of the city of London for provisions for three lunar months. Bread, biscuits, butter, to be issued on one day with porridge, on the next day with peas.

MOUNTJOY My lord, I beg you, I've read these lists so often that they begin to turn my stomach.

CECIL Yes. Yes. Of course. It is, you must admit, a first-class piece of organisation —

MOUNTJOY (*Bowing slightly*) Agreed.

CECIL Remarkable, really, the resources of modern warfare.

MOUNTJOY No one knows better than I how efficient our war department can be.

CECIL You're quite sure you feel fully prepared?

MOUNTJOY Quite sure.

CECIL There isn't anything else I can —

MOUNTJOY Nothing, my lord. I have moved myself on to a high place as required by my command. I can see further. I can look down. And I know the distance I have come to get this far.

CECIL You must not feel in any way distressed —

MOUNTJOY I do not.

CECIL The man in public affairs, my dear Mountjoy, is always divided, and to keep one's sanity one has to keep this division perfectly clear at all times. We must not bring the delicate distinctions of a private conscience into our dealings of state. It would be intolerable. Neither is there place in our private lives for the kind of power which we exert at our desks or on the battlefield. If I sign a death warrant I will not have the disembowelled offal of the wretch interfere with my taste for beef. Men in great places, as our cousin Bacon would say, gain power over others only to lose power over themselves. The man who cannot keep these two compartments separate is doomed. That is all.

MOUNTJOY I shall do everything I can. For the sake of my Queen.

CECIL But of course, of course. There is now another matter of immense gravity. I have been keeping it to the last.

MOUNTJOY Yes?

CECIL Our intelligence reports that the Spaniards have begun to move. A fleet under Aguila is said to be assembled at Lisbon. It is still but a rumour, of course.

MOUNTJOY Hah! Another rumour. You must breakfast upon rumours, my Lord Secretary.

CECIL My dear Mountjoy. I have survived this long because of my courtship of every tittle-tattle that shows her face. 'Open your ears; for which of you will stop the vent of hearing when loud rumour speaks.' My skill is in deciding which one to believe. And I believe this one.

MOUNTJOY Well let the Spaniards come! We are ready as the Lords of Admiralty were ready in '88. May the Almighty send us another storm at sea.

CECIL What is remarkable and to our advantage is that reports will insist that the Spaniard is headed for Cork.

MOUNTJOY And not the North?

CECIL Not the North.

MOUNTJOY O'Neill will have to cross the country to meet him.

CECIL Exactly.

MOUNTJOY This you may leave with me.

CECIL And I do so. (*Both rise*) Let us go to the Queen. By the way, talking of the Queen, we ought to compose ourselves carefully before we present these latest claims of O'Neill. She is already distracted in a terrible way at the mere mention of his name. She calls him at times her Golden Calf. At other times she cries out with the Sword of State in her hand that all have failed her but that she herself will corner him yet, her Great Running Beast —

Slow exit and fade-out. Music.

The road to Kinsale. Winter.

Well upstage on a low wall sit or crouch three spies. MOYLE *is head and shoulders above the other two who appear like extensions of his very person so closely do they squat together.*

MOYLE Christmas, the year of the Lord, 1601. We have come to a conclusion one way or the other —

O'FLANNIGAN (*In a kind of stupor*) Ireland has waited a long time for this day —

MOYLE (*Pompously*) It is time we considered our situation. Let us briefly consider the odds on either side of the battle. For we have to survive, do we not, whoever wins the day? I mean to say — we do not aspire to being martyrs. Are we any different to anyone else? In fifty years it won't matter to us one way or the other. We are only giving voice to the people of the earth — Let us then cast our experienced eye (if I may say so myself) over the field. Ah and what a field! What a setting for a magnificent combat!

MAHON (*Excitedly*) Mr Moyle, the Spaniards are still barricaded inside in Kinsale by the Deputy Mountjoy —

MOYLE Quite, quite —

MAHON Waitin' for O'Neill to come down from the North and lift the siege. They say the Spaniards are saying if he don't come quick they'll up and go off home again and lave (*leave*) the Irish to their own devices —

MOYLE This much every ploughboy in Munster knows already. No, I was not thinking of facts. But of tactics. A most interesting situation. The Spaniards in the town. Mountjoy surrounding them. And now — now — what do the Irish do? Hm? Fascinating —

O'FLANNIGAN (*Intoning*) Ireland has waited four hundred years for this day —

MAHON Is it that long now?

O'FLANNIGAN Over four hundred years since the English first settled here. (*Pause*) It's a long time to sit on the side of the road waiting for the Prince to pass by.

MAHON But he's coming now! He'll drive the foreigners into the say (*sea*)!

O'FLANNIGAN (*He seems to be possessed by a voice not his own*) And everything will be the same again as it was in the Golden Age. The cow will carry milk then in the worst of winters. The stalk will bend under the weight of a corn.

MAHON Aye. It'll surely be a time of marvels when the Irish are their own masters again.

MOYLE (*With an admonitory cough*) Gentlemen! Gentlemen! Please! Let's not jump to conclusions. In all my years of public affairs I have learned one lesson: things are never what they seem to be, and if they are, they shouldn't be.

O'FLANNIGAN (*Hysterically*) The day has come! The day has come!

MOYLE (*Tapping him on the shoulder*) You've turned out a poor sort of a spy, Flannigan. It amazes me that I continue to employ you. But in these difficult times one's resources are limited —

O'FLANNIGAN (*Jumping to his feet*) I'm telling ya, it's the hour! Let every Irishman worth his salt stand up and be counted!

MOYLE (*Coldly*) Mahon, give your report again of the state of the locality so that this idiot may learn sense. How do the local chieftains stand? Are they wavering? How many of them have already gone over to the side of Mountjoy?

MAHON (*Memorising*) There's an O'Brien of Thomond. A MacCarthy of Muskerry with Mountjoy already —

O'FLANNIGAN May the groan of birth be the groan of death to them —

MOYLE Indeed. And there's more, much more but I don't waste time —

O'FLANNIGAN But the saviour is coming out of the North! O'Neill is on the way South with all the Northern chieftains —

MOYLE And what does he leave behind him, you fool! Half the country studded with English forts. A great steel trap to catch the bear's head. And for every Irishman that marches with O'Neill there are two at home ready to stab him in the back —

MAHON Sure isn't Niall Garve O'Donnell already burning half of Ulster on behalf of the English.

MOYLE Precisely!

MAHON God Almighty save us! Look at the destruction that's been brought down on our heads for nothing at all. What's to become of us at all and our bits of property?

Slowly in the distance the beat of a drum. It gets louder in the following dialogue.

MOYLE (*Finger up*) Sh!

MAHON What is it?

MOYLE O'Neill.

They listen.

MAHON Mr Moyle. Mr Moyle, sir —

MOYLE Yes.

MAHON Tell us — what side are we on —

MOYLE Does it matter in the end? As a public servant I can only do my duty whoever is master —

The drums are nearer now.

MAHON But Mr Moyle, what are we going to do? We'd better do something quick —

MOYLE What are we going to do? We're going to sit on the ditch and wait. It is too early yet to be patriots.

O'FLANNIGAN sinks down beside him. The lights are lowered on the trio but a silhouette is retained. Across the forestage march O'NEILL, CORMAC, CLANSMEN, and POET, MOUNTFORT, his clerics and banner. They are all muffled against the cold.

O'NEILL We'll wait here for Art before going any further.

They take up positions around him.

POET (*Chanting*) Not since the journey of another O'Neill, Muirceartach King of Aileach, Muirceartach of the Leather Coats, son of Niall Glundubh, has a winter march through Ireland been made the likes of this one of Hugh.

Enter ART.

O'NEILL Well, Art, did O'Donnell get through safely without them cutting him off?

ART He got here quicker than you did. What in the name of heaven kept you? God, man, it's seven weeks since you began to move in Ulster. Who'd blame the Spaniards if they went home. Then the reputation of the O'Neills'd be gone forever. We wouldn't be able to hold our heads up again in a hurry.

O'NEILL You fool! Don't you know that we're in the most dangerous position we've ever been in in our lives?

ART Listen here. There are six thousand Irishmen out there around Kinsale. Together with the Spaniards we are more than all the English in Ireland. And yer man Mountjoy is caught in between us. And you talk of danger! Christ, we should be down there now, fighting for Ireland.

O'NEILL God, man, can't you and your likes ever face facts? If we had twenty thousand men, we'd still be inferior to the English.

ART No Irishman is inferior to an Englishman.

O'NEILL I repeat. We have a scattered army of wild raiders who carry what food they have in their pockets. And we are faced by a disciplined, professional army. One charge from the English could send us running.

ART Insults! Talk! Talk! Well let me tell you the message from O'Donnell. He says he's going ahead without you if you don't move now.

CORMAC   There is some sense in it, Hugh. December is no
         month to be sitting around in the open. The men
         will freeze!

ART   Come on outta that! What are we waiting for?

O'NEILL To starve Mountjoy out of his supplies. That's what
         we're waiting for. He is caught now between us
         and the Spaniards. If possible we will not open a
         single wound.

ART   God Almighty, you've gone soft. (*To the* CLANS-
         MEN) He's gone soft, can't ye see? Have we marched
         three hundred miles to hear the talk of an auld
         woman who's afraid of blood? (*To* O'NEILL) You
         talk of Mountjoy as if he were a sick child. Well to
         me he is not even an enemy. He is more. He is
         English. He is the brother of a rat and I will crush
         him or be crushed and have the same joy whatever
         the outcome.

O'NEILL (*Wearily*) You're a simple and a brave man, Art.
         Maybe I am soft. Maybe it's people like you who
         should lead rebellions, men of metal, and not just
         men of flesh and blood.

ART   (*Mollified*) Indeed and I'd do as well as the next
         man, now.

CORMAC   (*Urgently*) Hugh, Hugh. Stop this talk. You know
         perfectly well that you're the only one who can face
         Mountjoy.

O'NEILL We have lanced the great abscess, Cormac. All the
         madness of the country is pouring out on top of us,
         savagery and fear and greed.

CORMAC   I've never gone against you, Hugh, but Art is right
         this time, for once. We have to destroy Mountjoy.

ART   Mountjoy? Jaysus, sure he's only a shagging
         Englishman. A dandy. With more silks on him
         than a Frenchwoman.

         The men laugh at this.

O'NEILL We must have reason in everything we do. Reason!
         Cormac, I know something of this Mountjoy. He is
         slow, patient and methodical. One of your empire-

builders. A man without imagination, with one or two ideas in his head which he will never let go. It is the dangerous genius of the English. The slow, ruthless concern with details which everyone else has dismissed as trivial.

Dimming of lights. Spot on MOUNTJOY *stalking, caged like an animal, between his guns. He is followed about by a nervous secretary.*

MOUNTJOY How can they speak to me of an assault upon the Spaniards? With O'Neill out there! (*To* SECRETARY) Say this — that I spend my days repairing my positions. That I dare not — no, no, better change that — that I prefer to keep my cannon in readiness. Say that we have bribed an Irish chieftain, one Brian MacHugh Óg MacMahon, with whiskey. That he says O'Neill cannot restrain the Irish. That tonight is the night! (*To self*) My lords of the Privy Council don't know what they're talking about. Don't write down that, you fool!

SECRETARY No, sir. No, sir.

MOUNTJOY Just a minute. You may further say to my Lord Secretary that of my eleven thousand men in the list there are a mere six thousand standing. You may say desertions take place daily, hour by hour. And that the sickness is cutting us down. (*Quietly*) Dear God, let them attack tonight!

Black-out. Lights up on O'NEILL *and his party exactly as before*

CORMAC I understand that, Hugh. But you can destroy him.

O'NEILL But not like this, for God's sake. Not like savages. That would be no victory. We'd never be able to control what we had let loose. The Irish would start fighting the Irish then, like dogs after one bone. How are the men now, Cormac?

CORMAC They have passed in among the trees for shelter. They're sopping wet but raring to go. The captains are waiting for us below on the road.

ART And well they might wait. Are we going to stand around here all night, perishing, talking like auld women?

O'NEILL We can wait a little longer when we've waited a lifetime.

ART You mean you've waited a lifetime. No one else. Can't you strike now before it's too late? Instead of wasting more time?

O'NEILL Waste? For over thirty years I've prepared for this. Thirty years. I've moved slowly because we had a long way to go. And then I thought I saw the road out of this darkness.

ART It leads to Kinsale.

O'NEILL It leads far beyond Kinsale. (*In a rising voice, some of the old fire*) We can be the heirs of Charlemagne. Knights of a new, holy Roman Empire. We can salvage the best of our past among the leaders of a new, united Christian Europe. But first we have to know our shortcomings.

CORMAC Don't be hard on the men, Hugh. They will follow you anywhere.

O'NEILL Ah, Cormac, they have to do more. They have to see themselves transfigured. But how can I make them believe in this miracle when I can hardly believe in it myself?

ART Words! Words! There is a battle to be won.

O'NEILL And there is a battle to be lost, too. Don't you forget that, Art. And if we lose it there is nothing left. A darkness will descend upon Ireland. Think of all our kinsmen who are only waiting for our destruction to grab what we own. Think of the people without leaders, without aristocracy. They will go backward, having nothing but what is in the past. And they may take centuries to find a future.

ART That's enough. We'll fight the English first. Then we can talk words.

O'NEILL Defeating the English is only half the battle. After that the battle with ourselves begins.

ART I've had enough of this. If we don't march tonight

	I'm leaving to join O'Donnell and I can tell you there'll be a queer lot of the clansmen with me.
o'neill	You wouldn't dare, brother Art.
art	Wouldn't I though? I'm not going to let a crowd of Spaniards say that the O'Neills funked it when called to help.
cormac	He has reason, Hugh.
o'neill	Cormac! Would you seriously consider an attack in open and unfamiliar country? The men can't fight pitched battles.
cormac	The men will fight anywhere, Hugh. Besides it's hard to restrain them now. They've come three hundred miles. It's now all or nothing.
o'neill	Am I talking to myself?
art	We'll get the men ready to go down and meet O'Donnell.

Exit.

o'neill	(*Loudly*) Stop him! (*But* art *has gone*) Cormac, what is it that has taken hold of us? I can't make my words count anymore.
cormac	Hugh — we've come all this way — to fight.
o'neill	I believe it's finally caught up with me —
cormac	Hugh! (*Urgently*) Not now —
o'neill	I've known it. Oh, I've known it. That one day, I'd no longer be able to slip away like a fish before the net's drawn in. I've spent the better part of a lifetime dodging finality.
cormac	Hugh, you musn't show doubt to the men, not now.
o'neill	The rebellion belongs to brother Art and men like him. Men of metal. How simply they see it all! I can't match that. I remember too many things that might go wrong and I know of all the things that are wrong. I was born for small fights and the trickery of peace-making. (*To* mountfort) Well, Father Mountfort, and what is to be your share if we destroy the English?
mountfort	You've said it yourself already, O'Neill. A christian

state. A new Holy Roman Empire.

O'NEILL Hah! I'd enjoy trying to bargain with you, Father Mountfort. That I'd like. It'd be worth beating Mountjoy just to sit opposite you and see you wriggle your way into power. It'd be worth beating the English just to see how far you'd go, Father Mountfort, and whether I'd be able to stop you. Look what's at stake! (*Moving off*) We must fight to win, Cormac! We've the makings of great entertainment afterwards, among ourselves! To win!

> *Exit* O'NEILL, CORMAC, CLANSMEN, MOUNTFORT *and* CLERICS. *Black-out. A harsh sound of war. Lights up.* POET *to the side and three spies rising in the background. A rumble of battle in the distance.*

POET Manifest was the displeasure of God and the misfortunes of the Irish on this day at Kinsale. Countless was the loss, although the number killed was small. For the power and valour, prosperity and affluence, nobleness and chivalry, dignity and renown, hospitality and bravery, devotion and pure religion of Ireland was lost in that battle.

> *The* POET *sinks to the ground.*

MAHON (*Leaping up and running about*) Oh God Almighty, let us be off outta here, quick.

MOYLE (*Rising*) Keep calm! No panic.

MAHON The English aren't going to make any difference now between the Irish they'll catch on the roads.

O'FLANNIGAN (*Rising*) Well, begod, I know what I'm going to do. I'm going to get meself a quart of whiskey and a dry room, and balls to the lot of them!

MAHON C'mon will ye! C'mon.

MOYLE We will return peaceably to our houses like peaceful men, conversing with no one. Remember we're ordinary innocent people. We don't want trouble from anyone. Remember that.

The lights are lowered and the drums beat menacingly and then fall off sharply. Lights up on MOUNTJOY *between his guns. He looks off as there are sporadic sounds of distant battle which gradually die out. His* SECRETARY *sits half asleep at his feet.*

MOUNTJOY (*Slowly, to himself*) It's all over. (*To* SECRETARY) Wake up, boy. You need not send my last dispatch to London after all.

SECRETARY I'm afraid it's already sent, my lord.

MOUNTJOY Then we must send another. It's all over. They just broke and ran. It all ended with one cavalry charge. Extraordinary!

SECRETARY Quite extraordinary, my lord.

MOUNTJOY You may say that but for the fact that our horses were starving we'd have chased O'Neill to Dungannon.

SECRETARY Should we mention losses, my lord?

MOUNTJOY Losses. Hm. You'd better say one officer and a couple of dozen men. Now, the political situation. Right through the fighting, for some extraordinary reason, the Spaniards stayed put in Kinsale and are now leaving in disgust. I am certain that we have persuaded away the main body of O'Neill's followers — what else?

SECRETARY Lough Foyle, my lord.

MOUNTJOY Good boy! Lough Foyle is ours. That great hook through the nose which will finally land this giant fish.

SECRETARY Nothing more, my lord?

MOUNTJOY What? Ah, yes! Say this: Lord Secretary, you once said it is a rule of nature that the weak must give way to the strong. I now know what you mean. War reduces everything to two simple camps, the destroyer and the destroyed. You may tell the Queen I have succeeded. Oh, my dear Lord Cecil, this diseased climate! I have a gross chill in my bowels and my water has become discoloured. Whatever curious delight this expedition has

given me I welcome my return to England. To clean
linen and good beef, my lord! To England!

*Music and fade-out. Lighting to suggest bleak defeat.
Enter a straggling line of men, exhausted, wounded
and dying. They assist one another across the stage.*
o'neill *and* cormac *follow in a sorry group of*
clansmen. *Lighting, music and pace suggestive of
a funeral.*

o'neill (*Pausing*) Wasn't it from here we went down to
Kinsale?

cormac It was.

o'neill Is it true that Art is gone across to Castlehaven to
get a boat for Spain with O'Donnell?

cormac 'Tis.

o'neill Will they never give up?

cormac Maybe we should have gone with them.

o'neill No. We'll go back to Dungannon, if there's anything left of it now.

cormac *If* we get back. Remember we burned the land on
the way down. They'll be waiting for us on the way
back. Every mile of the road. Behind every scrap of
a ditch. (*Sudden explosion*) Goddamnit, I'd face the
Englishman five times over before I'd face the
milky half-Irish of the Midlands with their sly jabs
from behind and their craws full of beef!

o'neill They're our own people, Cormac, though they
don't know it. (*Wearily*) We started too early or too
late. I don't know which. We have to go on with
what's left to us.

Enter four clansmen *carrying a headless corpse.*

What's this?

The corpse is put down at his feet.

cormac (*Bending down to examine it*) Do you not know him?

o'neill How could I know him without the head? What're

they bringing him here for? Let them find the head and bury the two parts.

CORMAC It's Owen, son of Siobhán.

O'NEILL (*Pause*) You mean, my Owen.

CORMAC It's your son.

O'NEILL What was he doing here?

CORMAC He came down with Art.

O'NEILL I haven't seen him since he left us for her people. That's why I didn't know him, you see. I'd know him otherwise. How could I forget him. (*Brokenly*) How could any man forget his own son? Oh take him up, for God's sake, and find the head. If ye have to go into Kinsale, find the head. It'll not be worth ye'r while to come back without it. D'you hear? The head! The head!

CORMAC C'mon with me, Hugh. We'll go now.

> He leads O'NEILL off, who still shouts back towards the men 'The head!', 'Find the head, d'you hear me!' The four men stand motionlessly above the corpse looking after him and the lights are dimmed slowly.
>
> Lights up on Mellifont Abbey. A line of gothic arches at the back end, the suggestion of stained glass from the wings. Downstage, snapped at the handle, stands the banner SPES NOSTRA, JESU ET MARIA, its cloth in tatters. A slightly raised platform centre-stage: an ornate chair on which sits MOUNTJOY. He is clad in the full regalia of his Lord Deputyship and is attended by two members of his council. Upstage, on the apron, sits CECIL, beneath the Tudor crest. Both he and MOUNTJOY speak directly to the audience to suggest the distance between them.

CECIL We have to believe that we can do something to determine our own future. Some people talk about fate or destiny but it is the talk of someone not quite in touch with the times. The new man of our day is a different fellow. I myself may be excused if I say that I've made my own small contribution, following in the footsteps of my late, esteemed father, of course —

MOUNTJOY Of course —

CECIL Ours is a troubled age but we may combat its worst excesses with efficiency. Organisation, planning, control. We have now established a system which virtually runs itself.

MOUNTJOY Your presence is irreplaceable, my lord.

CECIL No, no, no. I am the great clerk. I write on paper. Our fashionable people at court may scorn this function but this does not perturb me. I will pass on my records to my replacement when I am called by the Divinity to make my own accountancy —

MOUNTJOY There is something troubling you, my lord.

CECIL The Queen is dead.

> MOUNTJOY *rises slightly in shock and slowly re-seats himself.*

Even at the end it seemed she would defy Death as she had defied so many of her living enemies. When I besought her that she must take to her bed, she smiled. 'Little man, little man,' she whispered, 'must is a word not to be used to princes.'

MOUNTJOY And now — she is dead!

CECIL There is no need for concern. The state has been well provided for. All opposition has been effectively destroyed. We mourn the passing of a great queen, yes, but her imperial monument will outlive all of us.

> *Pause.*

You've chosen an odd place, this Mellifont Abbey, to receive the submission of O'Neill?

MOUNTJOY It was chosen with some care, my lord.

CECIL You mean the old religion and the old Gaelic system —

MOUNTJOY I mean it as an emblem to the people. The stamping out of the old religion and the stamping out of the old tribal system, in one.

CECIL   Her majesty would have savoured the idea. My only regret is that she did not live to see O'Neill like this.

As he speaks, O'NEILL *enters upstage and kneels, to the side, outside the main room.*

MOUNTJOY   (*Looking off*) Yes. In the end they enjoyed a kind of fierce kinship.

CECIL   (*Briskly*) Now, my lord. O'Neill must be told nothing of the death of Her Majesty until he has submitted with full humility. The death of the Queen might prompt him to fresh pride, seeing that they had been violently opposed for so long. One can never be too sure with those Irish. Their cause may be burned out but I would leave nothing there to smoulder.

MOUNTJOY   There's nothing to smoulder. It's all over. The country is a threadbare polished garment and O'Neill a beggarman on his knees. (*Fade out* CECIL) Very well then. Let us have O'Neill in!

COUNCILLOR   Let the Earl of Tyrone enter into the presence of the Lord Deputy.

O'NEILL *enters.*

MOUNTJOY   Now, Lord Tyrone, let's try to dispose of this business as quickly as possible.

O'NEILL   There are just one or two questions —

MOUNTJOY   I want no supplications —

O'NEILL   Lord Deputy, I've always, up to most recent times, been a loyal subject of the Queen.

MOUNTJOY   My dear O'Neill —

O'NEILL   Isn't it true that Her Majesty in times past confided in me?

MOUNTJOY   We're not talking of times past, man. (*Pause*) I take it you've prepared your submission along the lines agreed to?

O'NEILL   I've prepared the wording exactly as you demanded.

MOUNTJOY   Well, then. Let's have it.

O'NEILL Lord Deputy —

MOUNTJOY Yes?

O'NEILL I simply wanted to ask how — what her Majesty has decided for the country.

MOUNTJOY Her Majesty — Her Majesty's Government may now do with the country as it thinks fit.

O'NEILL Her Majesty will nevertheless value the loyalty of the native Irish that remain.

MOUNTJOY Look here, O'Neill, for the first time in history every acre of this island is properly under the control of the Crown. Don't you know what this means?

O'NEILL I'll go to London! I'll speak before the throne itself. I know my word will be believed. Haven't I done good service in the past? Didn't I fight Maguire for the Queen in '93? You don't understand the nature of this rebellion. But the Queen — the Queen, she'll understand.

The way of O'NEILL *is barred by men.*

MOUNTJOY You will stay here until you submit.

O'NEILL Alright. So! What am I promised on the strength of this submission, Lord Deputy?

MOUNTJOY A pardon in the name of the Queen. Your restoration to the title Earl of Tyrone. That is all.

O'NEILL Do you think Her Majesty will leave us O'Neills our lands?

MOUNTJOY You've heard my words.

O'NEILL And what weight do they carry?

MOUNTJOY Come, my dear fellow, let's be sensible about these things.

O'NEILL I can't return to Ulster and remain alive on words. You don't know the place.

MOUNTJOY You've been a rebel. What do you expect?

O'NEILL For myself? Nothing. Not a thing. But there are still two or three dozen — no more — a few faithful people bound to me by blood and love. I'm pleading for these.

MOUNTJOY It is not in the interest of the Queen for any man in

71

this country to retain followers.

O'NEILL Followers! 'Tisn't an army we're talking about. These are the remains of a great tribe, not the beginning of a new one. They have no sustenance but what they can find through me.

MOUNTJOY That is the penalty of defeat.

O'NEILL God, man, don't you understand?

MOUNTJOY I understand that any power in this land other than the Queen's power is outrageous and a threat to law and order.

O'NEILL Power? Who's talking about power? I want no power, believe me. I've had my bellyful of that. And of the flood of madness which it lets loose. I have a simple responsibility as of — father to son. Just like that. These are simple people. Why must they suffer? They are only the old men, women, and the children.

MOUNTJOY They are all O'Neills, aren't they?

O'NEILL (*In a whisper*) You are goading me.

MOUNTJOY Sir, I am responsible for the security of the kingdom.

O'NEILL You have your security! O'Donnell poisoned. The clans scattered. Master Mountfort griddled over a slow fire. Security! Nothing could be more secure than a dead man, a dead country.

MOUNTJOY We have brought the war to its logical conclusion. No more.

O'NEILL For God's sake leave us our self-respect. It is very little to ask.

MOUNTJOY You are in no position to ask for anything.

O'NEILL I will not be a complete beggarman, d'you hear!

MOUNTJOY You have still to make your submission, my lord.

O'NEILL You've chosen well, Lord Deputy, this Abbey of Mellifont. At the consecration of this place the High King, the Kings of Ulster, of Oriel and of Breiffne, all came laden with their gifts.

MOUNTJOY Really?

O'NEILL Now the monastery houses a Protestant knight. The monks are ghosts and there are no kings in Oriel or Breiffne.

MOUNTJOY   Nor in Ulster. Do you think we might have your submission now?

O'NEILL   (*Reading carelessly*) I, Hugh, Earl of Tyrone, do now —

MOUNTJOY   It is customary to kneel, my lord.

O'NEILL *kneels before him.*

O'NEILL   (*The reading is in a dead monotone*) I, Hugh, Earl of Tyrone, do now appeal to the princely clemency of my Most Gracious Majesty Elizabeth. I ask that she mitigate her just indignation against me and my unnatural rebellion. I promise that, if Her Majesty in Her Royal generosity should see fit to restore me to my dignities, I will remain her loyal subject in the little time remaining to me of mortality. I abjure all foreign power especially that of the Kings of Spain. I resign all lands, titles, arms, and dependencies. Finally, I do promise to be advised by Her Majesty's magistrates, to aid them in the advancement of her service, and to assist in the destruction of all barbarous Gaelic customs —

Long pause.

Will Her Majesty honour my protection now?

MOUNTJOY   Her Majesty is — very lenient.

O'NEILL   I only wish to be left in peace now. I haven't a whole lot longer to live. I've already the taste of my own dust in my mouth. (*Dreamily*) Tell the Queen that Ulster is at peace again. Worn, spent, but at peace. Tell her that her Great Running Beast has been run to ground. The hunt is over. She can draw off her hounds. Silence her hunting horns.

MOUNTJOY   (*Loudly*) You must not press me like this. Can't you get into your head! It's all over. Finished! You've had your day!

O'NEILL   I'll leave you, my lord. I'll go back to my kinsmen. They need me, you know. I'm still O'Neill, am I not? My name has not been taken away from me. I

73

may not have two spears to support me but even in poverty I am still their Prince. (*Whisper*) O'Neill.

Exit slowly. Lights down slowly on MOUNTJOY *who looks off.*